Tex Mex

Jo Richardson

Bath · New York · Singapore · Hong Kong · Cologne · Delhi · Melbourne

This edition published by Parragon in 2009

Parragon
Queen Street House
4 Queen Street
Bath BA1 1HE, UK

Created and produced by
The Bridgewater Book Company

Cover Design Ummagumma

Photographer Emma Neish
Home Economist Joy Skipper

ISBN 978-1-4075-6662-7
Printed in China

Notes for the reader
This book uses both metric and imperial measurements. Follow the same units of
measurement throughout; do not mix metric and imperial. All spoon measurements are level:
teaspoons are assumed to be 5 ml, and tablespoons are assumed to be 15 ml. Unless otherwise
stated, milk is assumed to be full fat, eggs and individual vegetables such as carrots are medium,
and pepper is freshly ground black pepper.

The times given for each recipe are an approximate guide only. The preparation times may differ
according to the techniques used by different people and the cooking times may vary as a result of
the type of oven used. Ovens should be preheated to the specified temperature. If using a
fan-assisted oven, check the manufacturer's instructions for adjusting the time and temperature.

Recipes using raw eggs should be avoided by infants, the elderly, pregnant women, convalescents
and anyone suffering from an illness.

CONTENTS

Tex-Mex, as its name reflects, is border food, gastronomically uniting Texas to the north with Mexico to the south. It is also a fusion food, embracing ancient Aztec, Spanish, Native American and cowboy influences.

Tortillas, refried beans, salsa, guacamole and soured cream – these are the staples of Tex-Mex cooking. Then there are the chillies, as in hot, hotter and hottest. However, in this book you will discover that Tex-Mex is not entirely about heat. Aromatic spices such as cumin combine with coriander, while sweet-scented cinnamon and dark plain chocolate add complexity to both savoury and sweet dishes.

Most of the recipes suggest a specific variety of dried or fresh chilli to use, but if you can't find these, use any hot or mild, fresh or

INTRODUCTION

dried chillies available. It is difficult to judge how hot a chilli will be from outward appearances, but as a general rule of thumb, the smaller the chilli, the hotter it is likely to be. The recipes direct you to 'deseed' fresh chillies before using, because this reduces their hotness, although the heat is actually contained in the membranes surrounding the seeds. You can, however, opt to leave the seeds in to produce a hotter result.

To reconstitute the delightfully smoky but very hard dried chipotle chilli, cook in boiling water for 5 minutes (the powerful fumes can irritate your lungs, throat and nose, so keep well away or protect your face), then leave to stand for 30 minutes, or until softened; other dried chillies can just be soaked in very hot water for 10–15 minutes. Always wear protective gloves when handling chillies.

There is strong emphasis on snacks in Tex-Mex cooking, with many characteristic dishes eaten with the fingers, encased in a tortilla or scooped up on a tortilla chip. This chapter features recipes for finger-food favourites such as quesadillas and empanadas, nachos and tostadas. But there's more to whet the appetite, including spicy soups, seafood specials and eggs prepared ranch-style.

STARTERS AND SNACKS

Mango, although lusciously fruity, goes wonderfully well with savoury ingredients and is enhanced, not masked, by the robust flavourings. The colour of its succulent flesh is an added bonus.

PRAWN AND MANGO COCKTAIL

INGREDIENTS

6 cherry tomatoes

1 large ripe mango

1 fresh mild green chilli, deseeded and
  finely chopped

juice of 1 lime

1 tbsp chopped fresh coriander

salt and pepper

400 g/14 oz peeled tiger prawns,
  cooked

fresh coriander, chopped, to garnish

ONE Place the tomatoes in a heatproof bowl and pour over enough boiling water to cover. Leave to stand for 1–2 minutes, then remove the tomatoes with a slotted spoon, peel off the skins and refresh in cold water. Dice the flesh and place in a large, non-metallic bowl.

TWO Slice the mango lengthways on either side of the flat central stone. Peel the 2 mango pieces and cut the flesh into chunks. Slice and peel any remaining flesh around the stone, then cut into chunks. Add to the tomatoes with any juice.

THREE Add the chilli, lime juice, chopped coriander and salt and pepper to taste. Cover and leave to chill in the refrigerator for 2 hours to allow the flavours to develop.

FOUR Remove the dish from the refrigerator. Fold the prawns gently into the mango mixture and divide between 4 serving dishes. Garnish with chopped coriander and serve immediately.

RECOMMENDED SERVINGS

*Serve topped with a spoonful of Coriander Mayonnaise
(see page 67). While you are preparing the mango,
whizz up a Frozen Mango Margarita (see page 87)
to put you in the mango mood.*

This elegant appetizer couldn't be simpler to make but requires several hours' chilling for the raw fish to 'cook' in the lime juice – you can tell that it's done when the fish turns opaque.

CEVICHE SALAD

INGREDIENTS

450 g/1 lb salmon, red snapper or
  sole fillets, skinned and cut into
  strips or slices
1 small onion, finely chopped
1 fresh jalapeño chilli or 2 small fresh
  mild green chillies, deseeded and
  finely chopped
juice of 3 limes
1 tbsp extra virgin olive oil

1 tbsp chopped fresh coriander, plus
  extra to garnish
1 tbsp snipped fresh chives or dill
salt and pepper
2 tomatoes, peeled and diced
1 ripe avocado, stoned, peeled and
  thinly sliced
2 tbsp capers, rinsed (optional)

ONE Place the fish, onion, chilli, lime juice, oil and herbs in a non-metallic dish and mix together. Cover and leave to chill in the refrigerator for 8 hours or overnight, stirring occasionally to ensure that the fish is well coated in the marinade.

TWO When ready to serve, remove the dish from the refrigerator and season to taste with salt and pepper.

THREE Arrange the fish mixture on a large serving plate with the tomatoes and avocado. Scatter the capers over the mixture, and sprinkle with chopped coriander to garnish.

NOTE

People with certain diseases (such as diabetes or liver disease) or weakened immune systems should never eat raw fish. The elderly and pregnant women (along with nursing mothers and young children) should also avoid eating raw fish.

RECOMMENDED SERVINGS

To make this dish more substantial, serve on a bed of mixed salad leaves. Alternatively, for a more traditional Tex-Mex meal, serve on top of shredded crisp lettuce with home-made Flour Tortillas (see page 51).

The richness of this tasty chilled soup is balanced by the sharp injection of lime and Tabasco. An optional dash of tequila adds an extra Tex-Mex kick.

CHILLED AVOCADO AND CORIANDER SOUP

INGREDIENTS

4 ripe avocados

1 shallot or 2 spring onions, finely chopped

850 ml/1½ pints cold chicken or strongly flavoured vegetable stock

150 ml/5 fl oz soured cream, plus extra to serve

2 tbsp tomato purée

few drops of Tabasco sauce, or to taste

juice of 1 lime, or to taste

1 tbsp tequila (optional)

1 tbsp chopped fresh coriander, plus extra to garnish

salt and pepper

ONE Cut the avocados in half lengthways and twist the 2 halves in opposite directions to separate. Stab the stone with the point of a sharp knife and lift out of the avocado.

TWO Peel, then roughly chop the avocado halves and place in a food processor or blender with the shallot, stock, soured cream, tomato purée, Tabasco, lime juice, tequila, chopped coriander and salt and pepper. Process until smooth, then taste and add more Tabasco, lime juice and salt and pepper if necessary.

THREE Transfer the mixture to a large bowl, cover and leave to chill in the refrigerator for at least 2 hours, or until thoroughly chilled.

FOUR Divide the soup between 4 chilled serving bowls and serve, topped with a spoonful of soured cream and garnished with extra chopped coriander.

RECOMMENDED SERVINGS

This is the perfect starter for an alfresco lunch or dinner Tex-Mex style. Follow with Tequila-marinated Beef Steaks (see page 39), cooked in moments on the barbecue. A pitcher of Sangria (see page 93) will complete the summery scene.

Stoke up your energy reserves with a bowl of this hearty soup – both comforting and sustaining. It is also highly economical as well as quick and easy to prepare.

BEEF AND BEAN SOUP

INGREDIENTS

2 tbsp vegetable oil
1 large onion, finely chopped
2 garlic cloves, finely chopped
1 green pepper, deseeded and sliced
2 carrots, sliced
400 g/14 oz canned black-eyed beans
225 g/8 oz fresh beef mince

1 tsp each of ground cumin, chilli
  powder and paprika
¼ cabbage, sliced
225 g/8 oz tomatoes, peeled
  and chopped
600 ml/1 pint beef stock
salt and pepper

ONE Heat the oil in a large saucepan over a medium heat. Add the onion and garlic and cook, stirring frequently, for 5 minutes, or until softened. Add the pepper and carrots and cook for a further 5 minutes.

TWO Meanwhile, drain the beans, reserving the liquid from the can. Place two-thirds of the beans, reserving the remainder, in a food processor or blender with the bean liquid and process until smooth.

THREE Add the mince to the saucepan and cook, stirring constantly, to break up any lumps, until well browned. Add the spices and cook, stirring, for 2 minutes. Add the cabbage, tomatoes, stock and puréed beans and season to taste with salt and pepper. Bring to the boil, then reduce the heat, cover and simmer for 15 minutes, or until the vegetables are tender.

FOUR Stir in the reserved beans, cover and simmer for a further 5 minutes. Ladle the soup into warmed soup bowls and serve.

RECOMMENDED SERVINGS

To make this snack more substantial, serve with a bowl of tortilla chips or warmed corn tortillas. Devotees of Tex-Mex cuisine may like to make a batch of home-made Flour Tortillas (see page 51) as an accompaniment.

Spice up your morning with these ranch-style or country-style eggs – an ideal dish for a weekend brunch. You can reduce the number of chillies if it's too early in the morning for a fiery hit.

HUEVOS RANCHEROS

INGREDIENTS

2 tbsp butter, bacon fat or lard

2 onions, finely chopped

2 garlic cloves, finely chopped

2 red or yellow peppers, deseeded and diced

2 fresh mild green chillies, deseeded and finely chopped

4 large ripe tomatoes, peeled and chopped

2 tbsp lemon or lime juice

2 tsp dried oregano

salt and pepper

4 large eggs

75 g/3 oz Cheddar cheese, grated

ONE Preheat the oven to 180°C/350°F/Gas Mark 4. Heat the butter in a heavy-based frying pan over a medium heat. Add the onions and garlic and cook, stirring frequently, for 5 minutes, or until softened. Add the peppers and chillies and cook for 5 minutes, until softened.

TWO Add the tomatoes, lemon juice and oregano and season to taste with salt and pepper. Bring to the boil, then reduce the heat, cover and simmer for 10 minutes, or until thickened, adding a little more lemon juice if the mixture becomes too dry.

THREE Transfer the mixture to a large, ovenproof dish. Make 4 hollows in the mixture and break an egg into each. Bake in a preheated oven for 12–15 minutes, or until the eggs are set.

FOUR Sprinkle with grated cheese and return to the oven for 3–4 minutes, or until the cheese has melted. Serve immediately.

RECOMMENDED SERVINGS

Choose from Tex-Mex traditional accompaniments, such as Flour Tortillas (see page 51), corn tortillas or tortilla chips, or conventional breakfast fare, such as toast or muffins to mop up the delicious sauce.

The quesadilla is the Tex-Mex take on a toasted cheese sandwich. Oaxacan cheese, also known as Asadero cheese, is the strictly authentic cheese to use, but mozzarella makes a good alternative.

CHORIZO AND CHEESE QUESADILLAS

INGREDIENTS

115 g/4 oz mozzarella cheese, grated
115 g/4 oz Cheddar cheese, grated
225 g/8 oz cooked chorizo sausage,
  outer casing removed, or ham, diced
4 spring onions, finely chopped

2 fresh green chillies, such as poblano,
  deseeded and finely chopped
salt and pepper
8 Flour Tortillas (see page 51)
vegetable oil, for brushing
lime wedges, to garnish

ONE Place the cheeses, chorizo, spring onions, chillies and salt and pepper to taste in a bowl and mix together.

TWO Divide the mixture between 4 flour tortillas, then top with the remaining tortillas.

THREE Brush a large, non-stick or heavy-based frying pan with oil and heat over a medium heat. Add 1 quesadilla and cook, pressing it down with a fish slice, for 4–5 minutes, or until the underside is crisp and lightly browned. Turn over and cook the other side until the cheese is melting. Remove from the frying pan and keep warm. Cook the remaining quesadillas individually.

FOUR Cut each quesadilla into quarters, arrange on a warmed serving plate and serve, garnished with lime wedges.

RECOMMENDED SERVINGS

Serve with a bowl of Guacamole (see page 59) and a salsa of your choice, such as Pico de Gallo Salsa (see page 61), Sweetcorn and Red Pepper Salsa (see page 63) or Pineapple and Mango Salsa (see page 65).

'Turnovers' do not sound quite so inviting as 'empanadas', but these puff pastry parcels are real winners. Their packaging makes them a great portable lunch or picnic food.

CHICKEN AND SWEETCORN EMPANADAS

INGREDIENTS

400 g/14 oz cooked chicken, diced

400 g/14 oz canned creamed-style
  sweetcorn kernels

1 small onion, finely chopped

8 pimento-stuffed green olives,
  finely chopped

2 tbp finely chopped fresh coriander

1 tsp Tabasco sauce, or to taste

1 tsp cinnamon

salt and pepper

350 g/12 oz ready-made puff pastry,
  thawed if frozen

plain flour, for dusting

beaten egg, for sealing and glazing

ONE Preheat the oven to 200°C/400°F/Gas Mark 6. Place the chicken, sweetcorn, onion, olives, coriander, Tabasco, cinnamon and salt and pepper to taste in a bowl and mix together.

TWO Roll out the pastry on a lightly floured work surface. Using a 15-cm/6-inch saucer as a guide, cut out 8 rounds.

THREE Place an equal quantity of filling on 1 half of each pastry round. Brush the edge of each round with beaten egg, fold the pastry over the filling and press the edges together to seal. Crimp the edges with a fork and prick the tops.

FOUR Place on a baking sheet, brush with beaten egg and sprinkle lightly with salt. Bake in the preheated oven for 20 minutes, or until golden brown and piping hot in the centre.

RECOMMENDED SERVINGS

Serve these empanadas either straight from the oven or cold with a salad garnish, such as strips of red pepper, shredded crisp lettuce and chopped onion. You can also serve them with a salsa of your choice (see pages 61–65).

Who can resist diving into a molten mountain of nachos and biting into that great combination of the soggy, chewy and crispy? Nachos are so easy to prepare, especially if you use canned refried beans.

NACHOS

INGREDIENTS

175 g/6 oz tortilla chips

1 quantity warmed Refried Beans (see page 55) or 400 g/14 oz canned refried beans, warmed

2 tbsp finely chopped bottled jalapeño chillies

200 g/7 oz canned or bottled pimentos or roasted peppers, drained and finely sliced

salt and pepper

115 g/4 oz Gruyère cheese, grated

115 g/4 oz Cheddar cheese, grated

ONE Preheat the oven to 200°C/400°F/Gas Mark 6.

TWO Spread the tortilla chips out over the base of a large, shallow, ovenproof dish or roasting tin. Cover with the warmed refried beans. Scatter over the chillies and pimentos and season to taste with salt and pepper. Mix the cheeses together in a bowl and sprinkle on top.

THREE Bake in the preheated oven for 5–8 minutes, or until the cheese is bubbling and melted. Serve immediately.

RECOMMENDED SERVINGS

The classic accompaniment to nachos is Guacamole (see page 59) and soured cream. Serve with an icy tumbler of Tequila Sunset (see page 89).

This is another Tex-Mex delight. Replace the pork mince with beef if you prefer and, to save time, use corn chips or nacho chips instead of the fried tortilla wedges.

PORK TOSTADAS

INGREDIENTS

1 tbsp vegetable oil, plus extra
  for frying

1 small onion, finely chopped

2 garlic cloves, finely chopped

450 g/1 lb fresh pork mince

2 tsp ground cumin

2 tsp chilli powder, plus extra to garnish

1 tsp ground cinnamon

salt and pepper

6 soft corn tortillas, cut into wedges

to serve

shredded iceberg lettuce

soured cream

finely diced red pepper

ONE Heat 1 tablespoon of oil in a heavy-based frying pan over a medium heat. Add the onion and garlic and cook, stirring frequently, for 5 minutes, or until softened. Increase the heat, add the mince and cook, stirring constantly to break up any lumps, until well browned.

TWO Add the cumin, chilli powder, cinnamon and salt and pepper to taste and cook, stirring, for 2 minutes. Cover and cook over a low heat, stirring occasionally, for 10 minutes.

THREE Meanwhile, heat a little oil in a non-stick frying pan. Add the tortilla wedges, in batches, and fry on both sides until crisp. Drain on kitchen paper.

FOUR Transfer to a serving plate and top with the pork mixture, followed by the lettuce, a little soured cream and diced pepper. Garnish with a sprinkling of chilli powder and serve immediately.

RECOMMENDED SERVINGS

Serve with a salsa (see pages 61–65) to add extra flavour, or make up a batch of Taco Sauce (see page 41) to spoon over the spiced pork. Enjoy with Classic Margaritas (see page 87) for a memorable 'happy hour'.

Here are some of the all-time Tex-Mex favourites, including fajitas, enchiladas and, of course, that legend in a bowl, chilli, in authentic border-style form, together with updates on the old classics, such as Spinach and Mushroom Chimichangas (see page 47) and Chilli-prawn Tacos (see page 41). There are other exotic seafood dishes, alongside that most traditional of Tex-Mex fare: beef steaks.

MAIN COURSES

PREPARE 15 minutes **COOK** 2½–3½ hours **SERVES** 4

This is a typical Tex-Mex-style chilli, with chunks of beef rather than mince and without beans. Purists would also omit the onions. The chocolate – a taste of old Mexico – gives extra depth to the sauce.

LONE STAR CHILLI

INGREDIENTS

1 tbsp cumin seeds

650 g/1 lb 7 oz braising steak, cut into 2.5-cm/1-inch cubes

plain flour, well seasoned with salt and pepper, for coating

3 tbsp beef dripping, bacon fat or vegetable oil

2 onions, finely chopped

4 garlic cloves, finely chopped

1 tbsp dried oregano

2 tsp paprika

4 dried red chillies, such as ancho or pasilla, crushed, or to taste

1 large bottle of South American lager

4 squares plain dark chocolate

ONE Dry-fry the cumin seeds in a heavy-based frying pan over a medium heat, shaking the frying pan, for 3–4 minutes, or until lightly toasted. Leave to cool, then grind in a mortar with a pestle. Alternatively, use a coffee grinder reserved for the purpose.

TWO Toss the beef in the seasoned flour to coat. Melt the fat in a large, heavy-based saucepan. Add the beef, in batches, and cook until browned on all sides. Remove the beef with a slotted spoon and reserve.

THREE Add the onions and garlic to the saucepan and cook gently for 5 minutes, or until softened. Add the cumin, oregano, paprika and chillies and cook, stirring, for 2 minutes. Return the beef to the saucepan, pour over the lager, then add the chocolate. Bring to the boil, stirring, then reduce the heat, cover and simmer for 2–3 hours, or until the beef is very tender, adding more lager if necessary.

RECOMMENDED SERVINGS

Serve with warmed Flour Tortillas (see page 51), or hunks of Chillied Cornbread (see page 53). Hand round a bowl of soured cream to douse the flames and wash it down with additional ice-cold beer of your choice.

This is a stew of southern climes rather than the chilly north, full of warm, sunny flavours. Mexican oregano is rather different to the Mediterranean variety, but the latter still works well here.

SPICY PORK AND VEGETABLE HOTPOT

INGREDIENTS

450 g/1 lb lean boneless pork, cut into 2.5-cm/1-inch cubes

plain flour, well seasoned with salt and pepper, for coating

1 tbsp vegetable oil

225 g/8 oz chorizo sausage, outer casing removed, cut into bite-sized chunks

1 onion, roughly chopped

4 garlic cloves, finely chopped

2 celery sticks, chopped

1 cinnamon stick, broken

2 bay leaves

2 tsp allspice

2 carrots, sliced

2–3 fresh red chillies, deseeded and finely chopped

6 ripe tomatoes, peeled and chopped

1 litre/1¾ pints pork or vegetable stock

2 sweet potatoes, cut into chunks

sweetcorn kernels, cut from 1 corn on the cob

1 tbsp chopped fresh oregano

salt and pepper

fresh oregano sprigs, to garnish

ONE Toss the pork in the seasoned flour to coat. Heat the oil in a large, heavy-based saucepan or flameproof casserole. Add the chorizo and lightly brown on all sides. Remove the chorizo with a slotted spoon and reserve.

TWO Add the pork, in batches, and cook until browned on all sides. Remove the pork with a slotted spoon and reserve. Add the onion, garlic and celery to the saucepan and cook for 5 minutes, or until softened.

THREE Add the cinnamon, bay leaves and allspice and cook, stirring, for 2 minutes. Add the pork, carrots, chillies, tomatoes and stock. Bring to the boil, then reduce the heat, cover and simmer for 1 hour, or until the pork is tender.

FOUR Return the chorizo to the saucepan with the sweet potatoes, sweetcorn, oregano and salt and pepper to taste. Cover and simmer for a further 30 minutes, or until the vegetables are tender. Serve garnished with oregano sprigs.

RECOMMENDED SERVINGS

Since this dish provides a cornucopia of flavour, plain boiled rice would make a suitable accompaniment. If, however, you are feeding unexpected guests, serve with wedges of Chillied Cornbread (see page 53).

Roasting the peppers, tomatoes, chillies and garlic enhances the flavour of this sumptuous seafood medley. You can use any other firm fish fillets or a mixture, if you prefer.

TEX-MEX SEAFOOD STEW

INGREDIENTS

1 each of yellow, red and orange
  peppers, deseeded and quartered
450 g/1 lb ripe tomatoes
2 large fresh mild green chillies, such
  as poblano
6 garlic cloves, peeled
2 tsp dried oregano or dried mixed herbs
2 tbsp olive oil, plus extra for drizzling
1 large onion, finely chopped
450 ml/16 fl oz fish, vegetable or
  chicken stock

1 lime, finely grated rind and juice of
2 tbsp chopped fresh coriander, plus
  extra to garnish
1 bay leaf
salt and pepper
450 g/1 lb red snapper fillets, skinned
  and cut into chunks
225 g/8 oz raw prawns, peeled
  and deveined
225 g/8 oz cleaned squid, cut
  into rings

ONE Preheat the oven to 200°C/400°F/Gas Mark 6. Place the pepper quarters, skin side up, in a roasting tin with the tomatoes, chillies and garlic. Sprinkle with the dried oregano and drizzle with oil.

TWO Roast in the preheated oven for 30 minutes, or until the peppers are well browned and softened.

THREE Remove the roasted vegetables from the oven and leave until cool enough to handle. Peel off the skins from the peppers, tomatoes and chillies and chop the flesh. Finely chop the garlic.

FOUR Heat the oil in a large saucepan. Add the onion and cook for 5 minutes, or until softened. Add the peppers, tomatoes, chillies, garlic, stock, lime rind and juice, chopped coriander, bay leaf and salt and pepper to taste. Bring to the boil, then stir in the seafood. Reduce the heat, cover and simmer gently for 10 minutes, or until the seafood is just cooked through. Garnish with chopped coriander before serving.

RECOMMENDED SERVINGS

Warmed Flour Tortillas (see page 51) would make a perfect accompaniment. For an additional touch of luxury, add a spoonful of the Coriander Mayonnaise (see page 67) to each serving of the stew.

This recipe features a famed sauce, Mole Poblano, renowned for its surprising pairing of chocolate and chilli. The result is sumptuous rather than strange, with a deep, rich, mellow quality.

CHICKEN MOLE POBLANO

INGREDIENTS

3 tbsp olive oil

4 chicken pieces, about 175 g/6 oz each, halved

1 onion, chopped

2 garlic cloves, finely chopped

1 hot dried red chilli, such as chipotle, or 2 milder dried chillies, such as ancho, reconstituted (see page 5) and finely chopped

1 tbsp sesame seeds, toasted, plus extra to garnish

1 tbsp chopped almonds

¼ tsp each of ground cinnamon, cumin and cloves

3 tomatoes, peeled and chopped

2 tbsp raisins

350 ml/12 fl oz chicken stock

1 tbsp peanut butter

25 g/1 oz plain dark chocolate with a high cocoa content, grated, plus extra to garnish

salt and pepper

ONE Heat 2 tablespoons of the oil in a large frying pan. Add the chicken and cook until browned on all sides. Remove the chicken pieces with a slotted spoon and reserve.

TWO Add the onion, garlic and chillies and cook for 5 minutes, or until softened. Add the sesame seeds, almonds and spices and cook, stirring, for 2 minutes. Add the tomatoes, raisins, stock, peanut butter and chocolate and stir well. Season to taste with salt and pepper and simmer for a further 5 minutes.

THREE Transfer the mixture to a food processor or blender and process until smooth (you may need to do this in batches).

FOUR Return the mixture to the frying pan, add the chicken and bring to the boil. Reduce the heat, cover and simmer for 1 hour, or until the chicken is very tender, adding more liquid if necessary.

FIVE Serve garnished with sesame seeds and a little grated chocolate.

RECOMMENDED SERVINGS

Spicy Rice (see page 57) adds colour and texture to this dish. Alternatively, serve with warmed Refried Beans (see page 55) and a bowl of Pineapple and Mango Salsa (see page 65) for a light finish to the dish.

PREPARE 15 minutes **COOK** 20–25 minutes **SERVES** 4

This is just about as light as it gets in Tex-Mex cooking – white fish fillets simply seasoned and baked, accompanied by a tropical fruit sauce enlivened with a dash of hot pepper sauce.

FISH FILLETS WITH PAWPAW SAUCE

INGREDIENTS

4 white fish fillets, such as sea bass, sole or cod, about 175 g/6 oz each, skinned
olive oil, for drizzling
juice of 1 lime
2 tbsp chopped fresh coriander
salt and pepper

lime wedges, to garnish
pawpaw sauce
1 large ripe pawpaw
1 tbsp freshly squeezed orange juice
1 tbsp freshly squeezed lime juice
1 tbsp olive oil
1–2 tsp Tabasco sauce

ONE Preheat the oven to 180°C/350°F/Gas Mark 4. Place the fish in a shallow ovenproof dish. Drizzle with oil and squeeze over the lime juice. Scatter the chopped coriander over the fish and season to taste with salt and pepper.

TWO Cover the dish tightly with foil and bake in the preheated oven for 15–20 minutes, or until the fish is just flaking.

THREE Meanwhile, to make the sauce, halve the pawpaw and scoop out the seeds. Peel the halves and chop the flesh. Place the flesh in a food processor or blender and add the orange and lime juices, oil and Tabasco to taste. Process until smooth.

FOUR Transfer the sauce to a saucepan and heat through gently for 3–4 minutes. Season to taste with salt and pepper.

FIVE Serve the fish fillets, in their cooking juices, with the sauce spooned over, garnished with lime wedges.

RECOMMENDED SERVINGS

Spicy Rice (see page 57), together with a touch of something rich and creamy, such as Coriander Mayonnaise (see page 67) make ideal accompaniments.

PREPARE 10 minutes, plus 2 hours' marinating
and 30 minutes' standing **COOK** 6–8 minutes **SERVES** 4

Now it's barbecue time, Tex-Mex style, with a marinade guaranteed to make your meat melt in the mouth. If the weather is looking less than favourable, then cook the steaks under a preheated hot grill.

TEQUILA-MARINATED BEEF STEAKS

INGREDIENTS

2 tbsp olive oil

3 tbsp tequila

3 tbsp freshly squeezed orange juice

1 tbsp freshly squeezed lime juice

3 garlic cloves, crushed

2 tsp chilli powder

2 tsp ground cumin

1 tsp dried oregano

salt and pepper

4 sirloin steaks

ONE Place the oil, tequila, orange and lime juices, garlic, chilli powder, cumin, oregano and salt and pepper to taste in a large, shallow, non-metallic dish and mix together. Add the steaks and turn to coat in the marinade. Cover and leave to chill in the refrigerator for at least 2 hours or overnight, turning occasionally.

TWO Preheat the barbecue and oil the grill rack. Let the steaks return to room temperature, then remove from the marinade. Cook over hot coals for 3–4 minutes on each side for medium, or longer according to taste, basting frequently with the marinade. Serve immediately.

RECOMMENDED SERVINGS

To add colour and texture to this dish serve with a bowl of Sweetcorn and Red Pepper Salsa (see page 63), and some crispy fried, pre-blanched potato slices or chunks. Serve with Classic Margaritas (see page 87).

This is a gourmet, not to say healthy take on a trusty Tex-Mex favourite – ideal for an informal dinner party. Use cooked prawns and just heat through gently in the sauce for an everyday option.

CHILLI-PRAWN TACOS

INGREDIENTS

600 g/1 lb 5 oz raw prawns, peeled
   and deveined
2 tbsp chopped fresh flat-leaved parsley
12 taco shells
spring onion, chopped, to garnish
taco sauce
1 tbsp olive oil
1 onion, finely chopped
1 green pepper, deseeded and diced
1–2 fresh hot green chillies, such
   as jalapeño, deseeded and finely
   chopped

3 garlic cloves, crushed
1 tsp ground cumin
1 tsp ground coriander
1 tsp soft light brown sugar
450 g/1 lb ripe tomatoes, peeled
   and roughly chopped
juice of ½ lemon
salt and pepper
to serve
soured cream

ONE Preheat the oven to 180°C/350°F/Gas Mark 4. To make the sauce, heat the oil in a deep frying pan over a medium heat. Add the onion and cook for 5 minutes, or until softened. Add the pepper and chillies and cook for 5 minutes. Add the garlic, cumin, coriander and sugar and cook the sauce for a further 2 minutes, stirring.

TWO Add the tomatoes, lemon juice and salt and pepper to taste. Bring to the boil, then reduce the heat and simmer for 10 minutes.

THREE Stir in the prawns and parsley, cover and cook gently for 5–8 minutes, or until the prawns are pink and tender.

FOUR Meanwhile, place the taco shells, open side down, on a baking sheet. Warm in the preheated oven for 2–3 minutes.

FIVE To serve, spoon the prawn mixture into the taco shells and top with a spoonful of soured cream.

RECOMMENDED SERVINGS

Serve with a colourful combination of salsas, such as Pineapple and Mango Salsa (see page 65) and Sweetcorn and Red Pepper Salsa (see page 63). Finish with a pitcher of Sangria (see page 93).

The secret of fajita success lies in the marinating of the meat prior to quick cooking. It may take a little forward planning but very little extra effort for a far superior result.

CHICKEN FAJITAS

INGREDIENTS

3 tbsp olive oil, plus extra for drizzling

3 tbsp maple syrup or clear honey

1 tbsp red wine vinegar

2 garlic cloves, crushed

2 tsp dried oregano

1–2 tsp dried red chilli flakes

salt and pepper

4 chicken breasts, skinless, boneless

2 red peppers, deseeded and cut into 2.5-cm/1-inch strips

8 Flour Tortillas (see page 51), warmed

ONE Place the oil, maple syrup, vinegar, garlic, oregano, chilli flakes and salt and pepper to taste in a large, shallow dish or bowl and mix together.

TWO Slice the chicken across the grain into slices 2.5 cm/1 inch thick. Toss in the marinade until well coated. Cover and leave to chill in the refrigerator for 2–3 hours, turning occasionally.

THREE Heat a griddle pan until hot. Lift the chicken slices from the marinade with a slotted spoon, lay on the griddle pan and cook over medium-high heat for 3–4 minutes on each side, or until cooked through. Remove the chicken to a warmed serving plate and keep warm.

FOUR Add the peppers, skin side down, to the griddle pan and cook for 2 minutes on each side. Transfer to the serving plate.

FIVE Serve immediately with the warmed tortillas to be used as wraps.

RECOMMENDED SERVINGS

Serve with Guacamole (see page 59), soured cream, Pico de Gallo Salsa (see page 61) and shredded iceberg lettuce to put in the fajitas. Accompany with Refried Beans (see page 55) or Spicy Rice (see page 57).

This is a dish for those seriously committed to comfort eating. It would be equally effective with good-quality beef mince in place of the pieces of beef, if you prefer.

BEEF ENCHILADAS

INGREDIENTS

2 tbsp olive oil, plus extra for oiling

2 large onions, thinly sliced

550 g/1 lb 4 oz lean beef, cut into bite-sized pieces

1 tbsp ground cumin

1–2 tsp cayenne pepper, or to taste

1 tsp paprika

salt and pepper

8 soft corn tortillas

1 quantity Taco Sauce (see page 41), warmed and thinned with a little water if necessary

225 g/8 oz Cheddar cheese, grated

ONE Preheat the oven to 180°C/350°F/Gas Mark 4. Oil a large, rectangular baking dish.

TWO Heat the oil in a large frying pan over a low heat. Add the onions and cook for 10 minutes, or until soft and golden. Remove with a slotted spoon and reserve.

THREE Increase the heat to high, add the beef and cook, stirring, for 2–3 minutes, or until browned on all sides. Reduce the heat to medium, add the spices and salt and pepper to taste and cook, stirring constantly, for 2 minutes.

FOUR Warm each tortilla in a lightly oiled non-stick frying pan for 15 seconds on each side, then dip each, in turn, in the sauce. Top with a little of the beef, onions and grated cheese and roll up.

FIVE Place seam side down in the prepared baking dish, top with the remaining sauce and grated cheese and bake in the preheated oven for 30 minutes. Serve immediately.

RECOMMENDED SERVINGS

Serve with a garnish of shredded iceberg lettuce, finely chopped red onion and cubes of firm avocado, tossed in lime juice to prevent discoloration. Accompany with a salsa (see pages 61–65) and Refried Beans (see page 55).

PREPARE 20 minutes   **COOK** 35 minutes   **SERVES** 4

These crisp deep-fried parcels are universally appealing and are speedy to make. For an alternative meat filling, try the Lone Star Chilli (see page 29) topped with chopped onion and grated cheese.

SPINACH AND MUSHROOM CHIMICHANGAS

INGREDIENTS

2 tbsp olive oil

1 large onion, finely chopped

225 g/8 oz small mushrooms, finely sliced

2 fresh mild green chillies, deseeded and finely chopped

2 garlic cloves, finely chopped

250 g/9 oz spinach leaves, torn into pieces if large

175 g/6 oz Cheddar cheese, grated

8 Flour Tortillas (see page 51), warmed

vegetable oil, for deep-frying

ONE Heat the oil in a large, heavy-based frying pan. Add the onion and cook over a medium heat for 5 minutes, or until softened.

TWO Add the mushrooms, chillies and garlic and cook for 5 minutes, or until the mushrooms are lightly browned. Add the spinach and cook, stirring, for 1–2 minutes, or until just wilted. Add the cheese and stir until just melted.

THREE Spoon an equal quantity of the mixture into the centre of each tortilla. Fold in 2 opposite sides of each tortilla to cover the filling, then roll up to enclose it completely.

FOUR Heat the oil for deep-frying in a deep-fryer or large, deep saucepan to 180–190°C/350–375°F, or until a cube of bread browns in 30 seconds. Deep-fry the chimichangas 2 at a time, turning once, for 5–6 minutes, or until crisp and golden. Drain on kitchen paper before serving.

RECOMMENDED SERVINGS

Serve with a spoonful of Guacamole (see page 59) and soured cream, a little chopped, deseeded fresh tomato with chopped onion and a side dish of Spicy Rice (see page 57). Enjoy with a Tequila Sunset (see page 89).

No Tex-Mex meal would be complete without an array of extra dishes on the side and in this chapter all the essentials are featured to ensure success. There is a range of salsas, from fiery to fruity, to perk up your main course, spiced beans and fragrant rice to provide additional flavour interest, as well as tortillas and cornbread for mopping up all those delicious juices.

SIDE DISHES AND ACCOMPANIMENTS

Fresh, home-made flour tortillas are, unsurprisingly, rather more delicious than the shop-bought variety, but the latter definitely win over on convenience when required in other Tex-Mex dishes.

FLOUR TORTILLAS

INGREDIENTS

350 g/12 oz plain flour, plus extra
  for dusting
1 tsp salt
½ tsp baking powder

75 g/2¾ oz lard or white vegetable
  fat, diced
about 125 ml/4 fl oz hot water

ONE Sift the flour, salt and baking powder into a large bowl. Add the lard and rub it in with your fingertips until the mixture resembles fine breadcrumbs. Add enough water to form a soft dough.

TWO Turn out the dough on to a lightly floured work surface and knead until smooth. Divide the dough into 12 pieces and shape each into a ball. Cover with a clean tea towel and leave to rest for 15 minutes.

THREE Roll out 1 ball at a time, keeping the remainder covered, into an 18-cm/7-inch round. Stack the tortillas between sheets of non-stick baking paper.

FOUR Heat a griddle pan or large, heavy-based frying pan over a medium-high heat. Cook 1 tortilla at a time for 1–2 minutes on each side, or until lightly browned in places and puffed up. Serve warm.

RECOMMENDED SERVINGS

As well as playing a leading role in many Tex-Mex mainstays, flour tortillas are great with soups and stews such as Beef and Bean Soup (page 15), Tex-Mex Seafood Stew (see page 33) and Lone Star Chilli (see page 29).

This is authentic chuck-wagon fare that will satisfy any hearty appetite. If you fancy a cheesy version, add 85 g/3 oz grated Cheddar cheese to the mixture and sprinkle extra on top before baking.

CHILLIED CORNBREAD

INGREDIENTS

140 g/5 oz polenta

70 g/2½ oz plain flour

3 tsp baking powder

1 small onion, finely chopped

1–2 fresh green chillies, such as
    jalapeño, deseeded and chopped

4 tbsp corn or vegetable oil

125 g/4½ oz canned creamed-style
    sweetcorn kernels

225 ml/8 fl oz soured cream

2 eggs, beaten

ONE Preheat the oven to 180°C/350°F/Gas Mark 4.

TWO Place the polenta, flour and baking powder in a large bowl, then stir in the onion and chilli.

THREE Heat the oil in a 23-cm/9-inch heavy-based frying pan with a heat-proof handle, tipping the frying pan to coat the base and sides with the oil.

FOUR Make a well in the centre of the ingredients in the bowl. Add the sweetcorn, soured cream and eggs, then pour in the hot oil from the frying pan. Stir lightly until combined. Pour into the hot frying pan and smooth the surface.

FIVE Bake in the preheated oven for 35–40 minutes, or until a wooden cocktail stick inserted into the centre comes out clean. Cut into wedges and serve warm from the frying pan.

RECOMMENDED SERVINGS

This robust accompaniment needs a main course that measures up to its stature. Serve it with Lone Star Chilli (see page 29) or Spicy Pork and Vegetable Hotpot (see page 31).

Frijoles refritos, to give them their proper name, are simply a Tex-Mex must and, while you can depend on the canned variety, why not enjoy the real thing now and again?

REFRIED BEANS

INGREDIENTS

225 g/8 oz dried pinto beans, soaked
  overnight and drained
2 onions, 1 quartered and 1 chopped
1 chopped and 1 whole bay leaf
1 fresh thyme sprig

1 dried red chilli, such as ancho
3 tbsp olive oil
2 tsp ground cumin
85 g/3 oz Cheddar cheese, grated
  (optional)

ONE Place the beans in a large saucepan with the quartered onion, the herbs and chilli. Pour over enough cold water to cover and bring to the boil. Reduce the heat, cover and simmer gently for 2 hours, or until the beans are very tender.

TWO Drain the beans, reserving the cooking liquid, and discard the onion, herbs and chilli.

THREE Place two-thirds of the beans with the cooking liquid in a food processor or blender and process until roughly blended.

FOUR Heat the oil in a heavy-based frying pan over a medium heat. Add the chopped onion and cook for 10 minutes, or until soft and golden. Add the cumin and cook, stirring, for 2 minutes. Stir in the puréed and reserved beans and cook, stirring constantly, until the liquid reduces and the mixture thickens. Stir in the grated cheese, if using, and cook, stirring, until melted. Serve immediately.

RECOMMENDED SERVINGS

You can ladle these on the side, without the cheese, of many of the main courses in the book, such as the Chicken Mole Poblano (see page 35) or the Beef Enchiladas (see page 45).

side dishes and accompaniments **55**

Both full of colour and flavour, this is so much more inviting than plain boiled rice. Add some canned red kidney or black-eyed beans with the stock for a more substantial alternative.

SPICY RICE

INGREDIENTS

3 tbsp olive oil

6 spring onions, chopped

1 celery stick, finely chopped

3 garlic cloves, finely chopped

2 green peppers, deseeded
   and chopped

sweetcorn kernels, cut from
   1 corn on the cob

2 fresh mild green chillies, deseeded
   and finely chopped

250 g/9 oz long-grain rice

2 tsp ground cumin

600 ml/1 pint chicken or vegetable
   stock

2 tbsp chopped fresh coriander

salt and pepper

fresh coriander sprigs, to garnish

ONE Heat the oil in a large, heavy-based saucepan over a medium heat. Add the spring onions, celery and garlic and cook for 5 minutes, or until softened. Add the peppers, sweetcorn and chillies and cook for 5 minutes.

TWO Add the rice and cumin and cook, stirring to coat the grains in the oil, for 2 minutes.

THREE Stir in the stock and half the chopped coriander and bring to the boil. Reduce the heat, cover and simmer for 15 minutes, or until nearly all the liquid has been absorbed and the rice is just tender.

FOUR Remove from the heat and fluff up with a fork. Stir in the remaining chopped coriander and season to taste with salt and pepper. Leave to stand, covered, for 5 minutes before serving. Serve garnished with coriander sprigs.

RECOMMENDED SERVINGS

Serve as an accompaniment to Fish Fillets with Pawpaw Sauce (see page 37), or Refried Beans (see page 55) and Chicken Fajitas (see page 43).

There are as many versions of this dish as there are cooks, but a good result always depends on using quality, ripe avocados. Mashing rather than puréeing gives control over the texture.

GUACAMOLE

INGREDIENTS

2 large, ripe avocados

juice of 1 lime, or to taste

2 tsp olive oil

½ onion, finely chopped

1 fresh green chilli, such as poblano, deseeded and finely chopped

1 garlic clove, crushed

¼ tsp ground cumin

1 tbsp chopped fresh coriander, plus extra to garnish (optional)

salt and pepper

ONE Cut the avocados in half lengthways and twist the 2 halves in opposite directions to separate. Stab the stone with the point of a sharp knife and lift out.

TWO Peel, then roughly chop the avocado halves and place in a non-metallic bowl. Squeeze over the lime juice and add the oil.

THREE Mash the avocados with a fork until the desired consistency – either chunky or smooth. Blend in the onion, chilli, garlic, cumin and chopped coriander, then season to taste with salt and pepper.

FOUR Transfer to a serving dish and serve immediately, to avoid discoloration, sprinkled with extra chopped coriander, if liked.

RECOMMENDED SERVINGS

This relish teams well with soured cream and salsa in tortilla-based dishes, such as Chorizo and Cheese Quesadillas (see page 19), fajitas (see page 43) and chimichangas (see page 47).

This is the most famous Tex-Mex salsa, its name translating as 'rooster's beak', so-called, allegedly, because it was traditionally eaten between the thumb and forefinger, pecking-style.

PICO DE GALLO SALSA

INGREDIENTS

3 large, ripe tomatoes
½ red onion, finely chopped
1 large fresh green chilli, such as jalapeño, deseeded and finely chopped

2 tbsp chopped fresh coriander
juice of 1 lime, or to taste
salt and pepper

ONE Halve the tomatoes, scoop out and discard the seeds and dice the flesh. Place the flesh in a large, non-metallic bowl.

TWO Add the onion, chilli, chopped coriander and lime juice. Season to taste with salt and pepper and stir gently to combine.

THREE Cover and leave to chill in the refrigerator for at least 30 minutes to allow the flavours to develop before serving.

RECOMMENDED SERVINGS

This fiery salsa is especially good with tortilla dishes, such as Chorizo and Cheese Quesadillas (see page 19) and chimichangas (see page 47), or it can be spread over plain grilled and barbecued meat and poultry.

This salsa has lots of natural texture and a sweet-and-sour taste. Use a large fresh green chilli in place of the bottled chillies if you prefer, or use half a red onion instead of the spring onions.

SWEETCORN AND RED PEPPER SALSA

INGREDIENTS

450 g/1 lb canned sweetcorn kernels

1 large red pepper, deseeded and diced

1 garlic clove, crushed

1–2 tbsp finely chopped bottled
jalapeño chillies, or to taste

4 spring onions, finely chopped

2 tbsp lemon juice

1 tbsp olive oil

1 tbsp chopped fresh coriander

salt

ONE Drain the sweetcorn and place in a large, non-metallic bowl.

TWO Add the red pepper, garlic, chillies, spring onions, lemon juice, oil and chopped coriander, then season to taste with salt and stir well to combine.

THREE Cover and leave to chill in the refrigerator for at least 30 minutes to allow the flavours to develop before serving.

RECOMMENDED SERVINGS

Try serving this with the Chicken Fajitas (see page 43) or beef dishes, such as Tequila-marinated Beef Steaks (see page 39) and Beef Enchiladas (see page 45).

PREPARE 15 minutes, plus 30 minutes' chilling
COOK 0 minutes **SERVES** 4

Full of tropical fruit flavours, this exotic salsa provides a lively flavour contrast to robust savoury Tex-Mex fare. You could substitute a pawpaw for the mango for a slightly different taste experience.

PINEAPPLE AND MANGO SALSA

INGREDIENTS

½ ripe pineapple
1 ripe mango
2 tbsp chopped fresh mint
2 tsp soft light brown sugar
juice of 1 lime

1–2 tsp Tabasco sauce or Habañero
  sauce, or to taste
1 large tomato, deseeded and diced
salt

ONE Slice the pineapple, then peel the slices and remove the cores. Dice the flesh and place in a non-metallic bowl with any juice.

TWO Slice the mango lengthways on either side of the flat central stone. Peel the 2 mango pieces and dice the flesh. Slice and peel any remaining flesh around the stone, then dice. Add to the pineapple with any juice.

THREE Add the chopped mint, sugar, lime juice, Tabasco and tomato, then season to taste with salt and stir well to combine. Cover and leave to chill in the refrigerator for at least 30 minutes to allow the flavours to develop. Stir again before serving.

RECOMMENDED SERVINGS

Bring an extra touch of sophistication to the Chicken Mole Poblano (see page 35) with a spoonful of this salsa on the side. It will also add vibrancy to the Chicken and Sweetcorn Empanadas (see page 21).

Making your own mayonnaise is very straightforward, especially with a food processor or blender. The addition of a green chilli gives it that traditional Tex-Mex flavour.

CORIANDER MAYONNAISE

INGREDIENTS

1 egg

2 tsp prepared mustard

½ tsp salt

squeeze of lemon juice

2 tbsp chopped fresh coriander

1 fresh mild green chilli, deseeded and finely chopped

300 ml/10 fl oz olive oil

ONE Place the egg in a food processor or blender, add the mustard and salt and process for 30 seconds.

TWO Add the lemon juice, coriander and chilli and process briefly.

THREE With the motor still running, add the olive oil through the feeder tube in a thin, steady stream. The mixture will thicken after half the oil has been added.

FOUR Continue adding the remaining oil until it is all absorbed. Transfer to a serving bowl, cover and leave to chill in the refrigerator for 30 minutes to allow the flavours to develop before serving.

NOTE

Recipes using raw eggs should be avoided by infants, the elderly, pregnant women, convalescents and anyone suffering from an illness.

RECOMMENDED SERVINGS

This mayonnaise goes well with the Prawn and Mango Cocktail (see page 9). Try a spoonful with the Fish Fillets with Pawpaw Sauce (see page 37) or use it instead of the soured cream in the Chilli-prawn Tacos (see page 41).

To satisfy the inevitable desire for something sweet after a surfeit of Tex-Mex savoury dishes, choose from this special selection of baked puddings and cookies, traditional Mexican deep-fried fritters and chilled desserts. Along with luscious tropical and tangy citrus fruits, pecans and scented cinnamon, seductive plain dark chocolate also features strongly, as well as tequila and even chilli!

For drinks, think tequila. For tequila, think Margarita. And here is the definitive formula, along with a recipe for a frozen, fresh fruit variation. But tequila can also appear in a mellower mode, its mature, golden form teamed with tropical fruit and coconut milk to make a sumptuous cocktail, or combined with Kahlúa and cream to make a spectacular liqueur coffee.

DESSERTS, BAKES AND DRINKS

This silken dessert with its crunchy caramel topping is traditional in Mexico and is commonly known as 'flan'. The addition of chocolate makes it even more luxurious and tempting.

MEXICAN CHOCOLATE CRÈME CARAMEL

INGREDIENTS

115 g/4 oz granulated sugar
4 tbsp water
600 ml/1 pint milk
55 g/2 oz plain dark chocolate, grated

4 eggs
2 tbsp caster sugar
1 tsp vanilla extract

ONE Preheat the oven to 160°C/325°F/Gas Mark 3. Place a 1-litre/1¾-pint soufflé dish in the oven to heat.

TWO Place the granulated sugar and water in a heavy-based saucepan over a low heat. Stir until the sugar has dissolved. Bring to the boil, without stirring, and boil until caramelized. Pour into the hot dish, tipping it to coat the base and sides. Leave to cool.

THREE Place the milk and grated chocolate in a separate saucepan and heat, stirring occasionally, until the chocolate has dissolved.

FOUR Meanwhile, beat the eggs and caster sugar together in a bowl with a wooden spoon. Gradually beat in the chocolate milk. Add the vanilla extract. Sieve into the prepared dish.

FIVE Stand the dish in a roasting tin and fill the tin with enough hand-hot water to come halfway up the sides of the dish. Bake in the preheated oven for 1 hour, or until set. Leave to cool, then invert on to a serving plate. Leave to chill in the refrigerator before serving.

RECOMMENDED SERVINGS

Delicious on its own, perhaps with some chocolate curls for a special occasion, you could also serve it with some ripe berries, such as raspberries or blueberries, or even sliced banana for a comforting treat.

There are many variations of this easy pudding, called *capirotada*, which turns a loaf of bread into an irresistible dessert. You can use sieved cottage cheese in place of the Cheddar for a lighter version.

MEXICAN BREAD PUDDING

INGREDIENTS

55 g/2 oz butter, plus extra for greasing

350 ml/12 fl oz water

225 g/8 oz dark muscovado sugar

1 cinnamon stick, broken

1 tsp ground aniseed

55 g/2 oz raisins

10 small slices bread

85 g/3 oz shelled pecans, toasted
  and chopped

55 g/2 oz flaked almonds, toasted

175 g/6 oz mild Cheddar cheese, grated

ONE Preheat the oven to 190°C/375°F/Gas Mark 5. Generously grease an oven-proof dish.

TWO Heat the water, sugar, cinnamon stick and aniseed in a saucepan over a medium heat and stir constantly until the sugar has dissolved. Add the raisins and simmer for 5 minutes without stirring.

THREE Spread butter on to one side of each bread slice and arrange buttered side up on a baking sheet. Bake in the preheated oven for 5 minutes, or until golden brown. Turn over and bake the other side for 5 minutes.

FOUR Line the base of the ovenproof dish with half the toast. Scatter over half the nuts and grated cheese. Remove and discard the cinnamon stick from the raisin mixture, then spoon half of the raisin mixture over the toast. Top with the remaining toast, nuts, grated cheese and raisin mixture.

FIVE Bake in the preheated oven for 20–25 minutes, or until set and golden brown on top.

RECOMMENDED SERVINGS

Serve with single cream poured over for a mid-morning or teatime indulgence, with a cup of strong coffee. Alternatively, hold the cream and serve with a glass of Tex-Mex Coffee (see page 95) for a dinner-time finale.

desserts, bakes and drinks **73**

This Tex-Mex-style doughnut is rather more appealing in appearance than its traditional relative, since the dough is piped into lengths, which twist into a variety of interesting shapes when deep-fried.

CHURROS

INGREDIENTS

225 ml/8 fl oz water
85 g/3 oz butter or lard, diced
2 tbsp dark muscovado sugar
finely grated rind of 1 small orange
  (optional)
pinch of salt
175 g/6 oz plain flour, well sifted

1 tsp ground cinnamon, plus extra
  for dusting
1 tsp vanilla extract
2 eggs
vegetable oil, for deep-frying
caster sugar, for dusting

ONE Heat the water, butter, brown sugar, orange rind, if using, and salt in a heavy-based saucepan over a medium heat until the butter has melted.

TWO Add the flour, all at once, the cinnamon and vanilla extract, then remove the saucepan from the heat and beat rapidly until the mixture pulls away from the side of the saucepan.

THREE Leave to cool slightly, then beat in the eggs, one at a time, beating well after each addition, until the mixture is thick and smooth. Spoon into a piping bag fitted with a wide star nozzle.

FOUR Heat the oil for deep-frying in a deep-fryer or deep saucepan to 180°–190°C/350°–375°F, or until a cube of bread browns in 30 seconds. Pipe 13-cm/5-inch lengths about 7.5 cm/3 inches apart into the oil. Deep-fry for 2 minutes on each side, or until golden brown. Remove with a slotted spoon and drain on kitchen paper.

FIVE Dust the churros with caster sugar and cinnamon and serve.

RECOMMENDED SERVINGS

Served either hot from the saucepan or cooled to room temperature, Churros go well with a cup of hot chocolate. They also make an elegant nibble with ordinary coffee or the Tex-Mex Coffee (see page 95).

These traditional, plain sweet fritters are served with their own flavoured syrup in which they can be dunked or drenched. Maple syrup, golden syrup or honey are good alternatives.

BUNUELOS WITH ORANGE-CINNAMON SYRUP

INGREDIENTS

225 g/8 oz plain flour, plus extra for
  dusting
1 tsp baking powder
¼ tsp salt
1 tbsp dark muscovado sugar
1 egg, beaten
2 tbsp butter, melted
about 125 ml/4 fl oz evaporated milk
vegetable oil, for deep-frying

orange-cinnamon syrup
350 ml/12 fl oz water
grated rind of 1 small orange
4 tbsp freshly squeezed orange juice
100 g/3½ oz dark muscovado sugar
1 tbsp clear honey
2 tsp ground cinnamon

ONE Sift the flour, baking powder and salt together into a large bowl. Stir in the sugar. Beat in the egg and butter with enough evaporated milk to form a soft, smooth dough.

TWO Shape the dough into 8 balls. Cover and leave to rest for 30 minutes.

THREE Meanwhile, to make the syrup, place the water, orange rind and juice, sugar, honey and cinnamon in a heavy-based saucepan over a medium heat. Bring to the boil, stirring constantly, then reduce the heat and simmer gently for 20 minutes, or until thickened.

FOUR Flatten the dough balls to make cakes. Heat the oil for deep-frying in a deep-fryer or deep saucepan to 180–190°C/350–375°F, or until a cube of bread browns in 30 seconds. Deep-fry the bunuelos in batches for 4–5 minutes, turning once, or until golden brown and puffed. Remove with a slotted spoon and drain on kitchen paper. Serve with the syrup spooned over.

RECOMMENDED SERVINGS

Serve these tempting fritters as a coffee-time sweet treat, or team with Tex-Mex Coffee (see page 95) for a late night feast. They would also make a great dessert with scoops of good-quality vanilla ice cream.

When you want to chill out, literally, this ice-cold dessert will hit the spot. It couldn't be more elegant. To add a finishing touch, decorate with lime slices or twists or finely pared strips of rind.

GUAVA, LIME AND TEQUILA SORBET

INGREDIENTS

175 g/6 oz caster sugar

425 ml/15 fl oz water

4 fresh ripe guavas or 8 canned
  guava halves

2 tbsp tequila

juice of ½ lime, or to taste

1 egg white

ONE Heat the sugar and water in a heavy-based saucepan over a low heat until the sugar has dissolved. When the liquid turns clear, boil for 5 minutes, or until a thick syrup forms. Remove the saucepan from the heat and leave to cool.

TWO Cut the fresh guavas, if using, in half. Scoop out the flesh. Discard the seeds from the fresh or canned guava flesh. Transfer to a food processor or blender and process until smooth.

THREE Add the purée to the syrup with the tequila and lime juice to taste. Transfer the mixture to a freezerproof container and freeze for 1 hour, or until slushy.

FOUR Remove from the freezer and process again until smooth. Return to the freezer and freeze until firm. Process again until smooth. With the motor still running, add the egg white through the feeder tube. Freeze until solid.

FIVE Transfer the sorbet to the refrigerator 15 minutes before serving. Serve in scoops.

NOTE

Recipes using raw eggs should be avoided by infants, the elderly, pregnant women, convalescents and anyone suffering from an illness.

RECOMMENDED SERVINGS

A refreshing dessert to serve after some of the heavier-duty starters and main dishes, it goes well with other dishes, such as the Ceviche Salad (see page 11) or the Fish Fillets with Pawpaw Sauce (see page 37) for a light meal.

Chocolate and chilli are a classic Tex-Mex combination with savoury dishes, but can also be used together in sweet dishes. The chilli just gives a warmth and richness to the chocolate.

CHOCOLATE CHIP AND CHILLI ICE CREAM

INGREDIENTS

1 egg

1 egg yolk

55 g/2 oz caster sugar

150 g/5½ oz plain dark chocolate, finely chopped

500 ml/18 fl oz milk

1 dried red chilli, such as ancho

1 vanilla pod

500 ml/18 fl oz double cream

150 g/5½ oz plain dark, milk or white chocolate chips

ONE Place the egg, egg yolk and sugar in a heatproof bowl set over a saucepan of simmering water. Beat until light and fluffy.

TWO Place the chopped chocolate, milk, chilli and vanilla pod in a separate saucepan and heat gently until the chocolate has dissolved and the milk is almost boiling. Pour on to the egg mixture, discarding the chilli and vanilla pod, and beat well. Leave to cool.

THREE Lightly whip the cream in a separate bowl. Fold into the cold mixture with the chocolate chips. Transfer to an ice cream machine and process for 15 minutes, or according to the manufacturer's instructions. Alternatively, transfer to a freezerproof container and freeze for 1 hour, or until partially frozen. Remove from the freezer, transfer to a bowl and beat to break down the ice crystals. Freeze again for 30 minutes, then beat again. Freeze once more until firm.

FOUR Transfer the ice cream to the refrigerator 15 minutes before serving. Serve in scoops.

NOTE

Recipes using raw eggs should be avoided by infants, the elderly, pregnant women, convalescents and anyone suffering from an illness.

RECOMMENDED SERVINGS

Reserve this rich dessert for serving after a middle-weight main course, such as the Tequila-marinated Beef Steaks (see page 39), Chilli-prawn Tacos (see page 41) or Chicken Fajitas (see page 43).

The name of these traditional Mexican cookies comes from the fact that they look like wedding bells, with their thick white coating of icing sugar. The nut halves can be chopped in a food processor.

MEXICAN WEDDING CAKES

INGREDIENTS

225 g/8 oz butter, softened

225 g/8 oz icing sugar

1 tsp vanilla extract

225 g/8 oz plain flour, plus extra
  for dusting

½ tsp salt

100 g/3½ oz pecan or walnut halves,
  toasted and finely chopped

ONE Cream the butter with half the sugar and vanilla extract in a large bowl. Sift the flour and salt together into the bowl and fold into the mixture. Stir in the nuts. Cover and leave to chill in the refrigerator for 1 hour, or until firm.

TWO Preheat the oven to 190°C/375°F/Gas Mark 5. With floured hands, shape the dough into 2.5-cm/1-inch balls and place about 4 cm/1½ inches apart on 2 large baking sheets.

THREE Bake in the preheated oven for 10 minutes, or until set but not browned, rotating the baking sheets so that the cookies bake evenly. Leave to cool on the baking sheets for 2–3 minutes.

FOUR Place the remaining sugar in a shallow dish. Roll the warm cookies in the sugar, then leave to cool on wire racks for 30 minutes. When cold, roll again in the sugar. Store in airtight containers.

RECOMMENDED SERVINGS

These make a cheering sweet snack for mid-morning or afternoon, are dainty enough to serve as part of a buffet-style meal and are also perfect after dinner with some Tex-Mex Coffee (see page 95).

Here we have a sweet alternative to the savoury empanadas on page 21, this time with a creamy, fruity filling and a hint of crunchy nut. You could use apricots or mangoes in place of the peaches.

PEACH AND PECAN EMPANADAS

INGREDIENTS

350 g/12 oz ready-made puff pastry,
  thawed if frozen
plain flour, for dusting
3 fresh peaches
150 ml/5 fl oz soured cream or
  crème fraîche

4 tbsp dark muscovado sugar
4 tbsp pecan halves, toasted and
  finely chopped
beaten egg, to glaze
caster sugar, for sprinkling

ONE Preheat the oven to 200°C/400°F/Gas Mark 6. Roll out the pastry on a lightly floured work surface. Using a 15-cm/6-inch saucer as a guide, cut out 8 rounds.

TWO Place the peaches in a heatproof bowl and pour over enough boiling water to cover. Leave for a few seconds, then drain and peel off the skins. Halve the peaches, remove the stones and slice the flesh.

THREE Place a spoonful of soured cream on one half of each pastry round and top with a few peach slices. Sprinkle over a little muscovado sugar and some nuts. Brush each edge with a little beaten egg, fold the pastry over the filling and press the edges together to seal. Crimp the edges with a fork and prick the tops.

FOUR Place on a baking sheet, brush with beaten egg and sprinkle with caster sugar. Bake in the preheated oven for 20 minutes, or until they turn golden brown.

RECOMMENDED SERVINGS

These pastries are best served warm. Serve as a snack or a dessert after a Tex-Mex main dish, such as Fish Fillets with Pawpaw Sauce (see page 37), to extend the fruity theme. Add some extra slices of fruit to decorate.

This is the drink that embodies the spirit of Tex-Mex – a fun-loving, sun-baked lifestyle served up in a cocktail glass. Besides the classic concoction, there are all sorts of fruit variations to be enjoyed.

MARGARITAS

INGREDIENTS

classic margarita

crushed sea salt

1 lime wedge

handful of ice cubes, roughly broken

3 tbsp tequila

3 tbsp freshly squeezed lime juice

1½ tbsp Cointreau

1 lime slice, to decorate

frozen mango margarita

caster sugar

1 lime wedge

½ mango, peeled and chopped

3 tbsp tequila

3 tbsp freshly squeezed orange juice

1½ tbsp freshly squeezed lime juice

handful of crushed ice

1 orange slice, to decorate

CLASSIC MARGARITA

ONE To make the Classic Margarita, sprinkle a layer of salt on to a piece of kitchen paper. Wipe the rim of a chilled cocktail or Margarita glass with the lime wedge, then invert on to the salt. Turn the glass upright, shaking off any excess salt.

TWO Place the broken ice cubes in a cocktail shaker, then add the tequila, lime juice and Cointreau. Shake well, then sieve into the prepared glass. Decorate with the lime slice and serve.

FROZEN MANGO MARGARITA

ONE To make the Frozen Mango Margarita, frost the rim of a large cocktail glass as in Step 1 of Classic Margarita but using sugar in place of the salt.

TWO Place the mango in a food processor or blender and process until smooth. Add the tequila, orange and lime juices and crushed ice and blend until well combined but still slushy.

THREE Pour into the prepared glass, decorate with the orange slice and serve.

RECOMMENDED SERVINGS

Enjoy a Classic Margarita with Salsa (see pages 61–65), soured cream and Guacamole (see page 59) and tortilla chips. Enjoy the Frozen Mango Margarita with warm sweet treats, such as bunuelos (see page 77).

Sultry sister to Tequila Sunrise, this is the ultimate cooler, fragrantly fruity yet with subtly discernible darker depths. And it looks every inch the part too.

TEQUILA SUNSET

INGREDIENTS

1½ tbsp white rum
1½ tbsp tequila
90 ml/3 fl oz freshly squeezed
  orange juice
1½ tbsp freshly squeezed lime juice

½ tall, straight-sided tumbler of
  crushed ice
1½ tbsp grenadine
pared spiral of lime rind, to decorate

ONE Place the white rum, tequila, orange and lime juices and crushed ice in a cocktail shaker.

TWO Shake briefly, then pour the cocktail, with the ice, into the glass used to measure ice.

THREE Sprinkle the grenadine on top. Do not stir. Serve, decorated with a spiral of lime rind.

RECOMMENDED SERVINGS

You can serve this drink with snacks such as Chicken and Sweetcorn Empanadas (see page 21) or Nachos (see page 23). It also goes well with main dishes such as Fish Fillets with Pawpaw Sauce (see page 37) or Tequila-marinated Beef Steaks (see page 39).

This creamy yet tangy fruity cocktail is a real Tex-Mex treat. Gold tequila is the standard drink matured in oak for a few years, during which time it mellows in flavour and turns golden in colour.

ACAPULCO

INGREDIENTS

1½ tbsp gold tequila

1½ tbsp dark rum

3 tbsp pineapple juice

1 tbsp freshly squeezed grapefruit juice

1½ tbsp coconut milk

½ Piña Colada glassful or tall, straight-sided tumbler of crushed ice

fresh pineapple wedges, to decorate

ONE Place the tequila, rum, pineapple and grapefruit juices, coconut milk and crushed ice in a cocktail shaker.

TWO Shake well, then pour, with the ice, into the glass used to measure the ice.

THREE Spear the pineapple wedges on to a wooden cocktail stick and place across the top of the glass. Serve with straws.

RECOMMENDED SERVINGS

A simple savoury or sweet snack goes well with it, such as dried corn tortilla wedges (see Pork Tostadas, page 25) or tortilla chips with Pineapple and Mango Salsa (see page 65) and soured cream.